Ham and Chicken Do Italy

By Kimberly Naylor
Illustrated by Lei Yang

Ii Jj Kk Ll Mm Nn Oo Pp Qq Rr Ss Tt Uu Vv Ww Xx Yy Zz

FACTS ABOUT ITALY:

1. Capital city: Rome
2. Money: the Euro
3. Italy as 3 active volcanoes: Vesuvius, Etna, Stromboli
4. Most popular sport: soccer "calcio"
5. Ancient Rome was the birthplace of a <u>republican/representative democracy</u>.
6. Italians invented the piano, thermometer, and PIZZA!

Football
Piano
Pizza
Volcano
Thermometer
Rome
Vesuvius
Stromboli
Etna

Let's learn something new about our <u>destination</u>. We think it will help us have a great vacation!

The facts are all here
and it says it on this line:
Italy's known as The Boot
because of its shape and design.

At the top of the boot,
sit the Alps like a fence.
They are a border between Italy
and Slovenia, Switzerland, Austria, and France.

France

See that part right there?
It looks just like the boot's toe-
from the clean and clear ocean
to the mountains with snow.

First we go to Rome
where all the fun starts-
ancient <u>ruins</u> and museums-
it's the center of the arts!

Here's the Colosseum,
an outdoor building that's round.
It's the biggest of all
amphitheaters around.

It once hosted fights
between gladiators and beasts,
pretend sea battles, dramas,
executions, and feasts.

The famous Roman Forum
is right here next door.
Often called the "Heart of Rome,"
citizens met here, rich and poor.

First used as a marketplace,
kind of like a store.
It then became a meeting place.
Ham, will you tell us more?

Let's go see the Pantheon!
It's over this way!
One of the best preserved <u>ruins</u>;
it's still in use today.

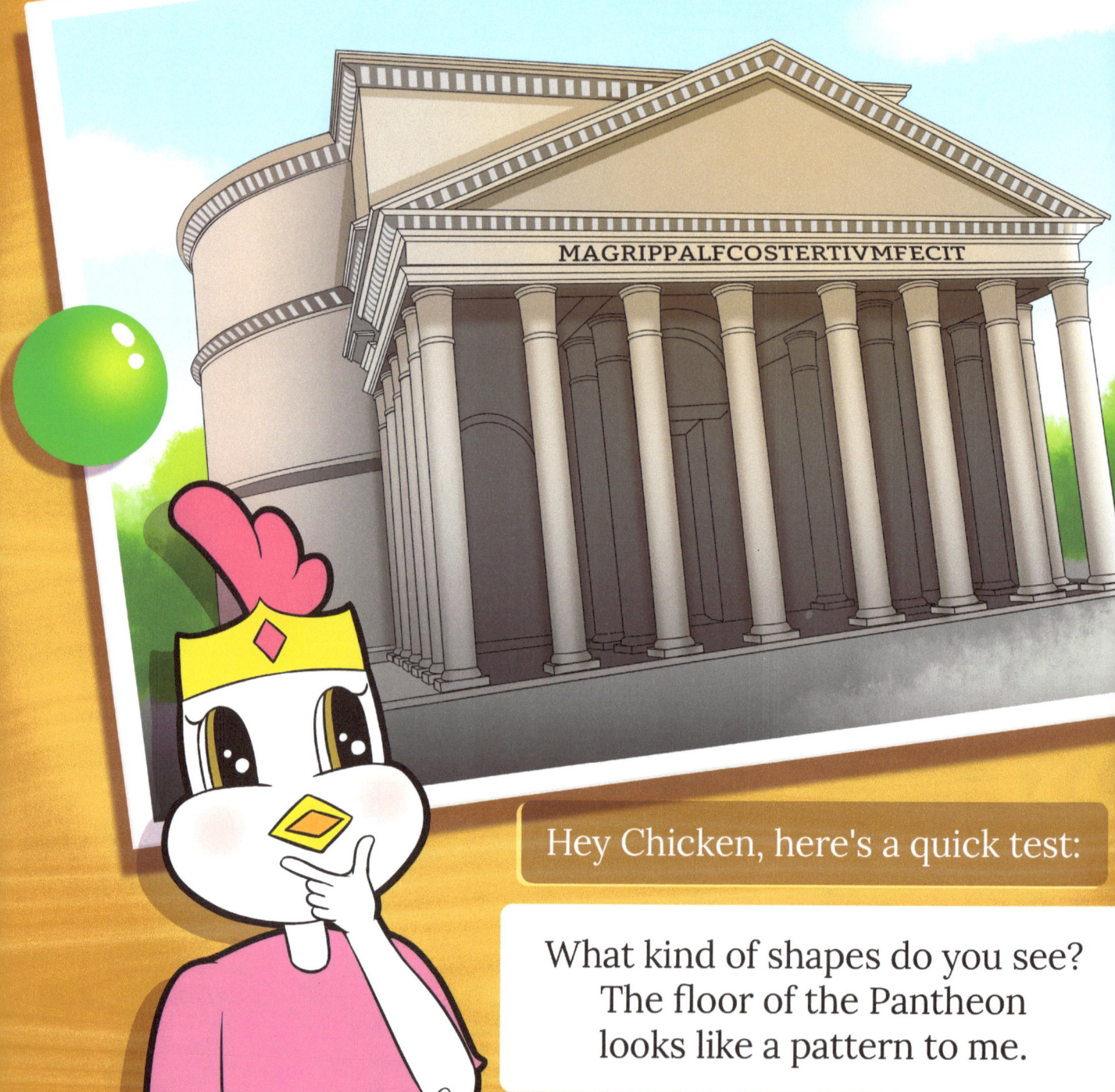

Hey Chicken, here's a quick test:

What kind of shapes do you see? The floor of the Pantheon looks like a pattern to me.

Next, let's see the Trevi Fountain.
We will get there real soon.
An army of seahorses
pulls mighty King Neptune.

Turn around and stand backwards.
Make sure to throw with your right hand.
Toss 3 coins over your left shoulder
and in the fountain they will land.

As legend will have it,
your wish will come true
as people from all over
the world have come here to do.

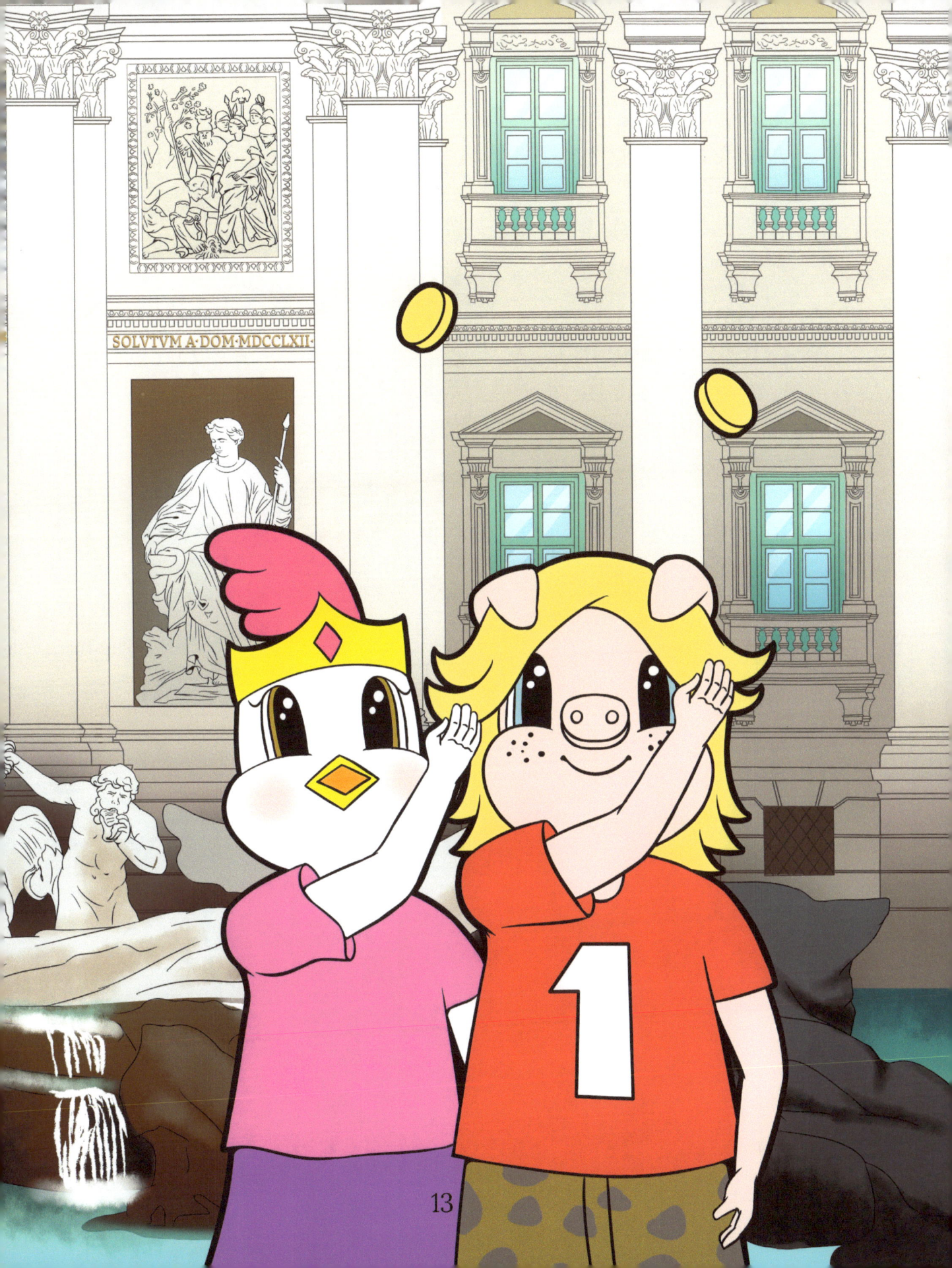

Do you know this fact?
We learned it just this minute.
Italy has two countries
sitting in the middle of it.

One is San Marino.
The other is Vatican City.
If you miss a visit here,
it sure would be a pity.

The Sistine Chapel ceiling
is the most famous one around.
Many bright colors were used
and is easily seen from the ground.

Michelangelo was the painter
who achieved this great <u>feat</u>.
It took 4 years of hard work
until the ceiling was complete.

He stood on <u>scaffolding</u>
to paint the great ceiling.
Imagine looking up that long!
I wonder how his neck was feeling.

Now we're off to Florence!
The Renaissance was born here.
It inspired art and culture
across Europe far and near.

The Renaissance was a time
people wanted to learn and do more.
They painted great pictures
and did science experiments galore.

This is the Medici family,
and let's be quite frank,
they made a lot of money
by owning a big bank.

They became the leaders.
They were the ones in charge.
During the Renaissance they ruled
and their power grew quite large.

They helped finance the Renaissance,
and we can't say it enough,
as patrons of art and science,
they paid for a lot of this stuff!

Do you know who this lady is?
Mona Lisa is her name.
A man of great talent
brought her half smile to great fame.

Leonard da Vinci!
Born right here in this city,
he was surely a genius.
Boy, was he smart and witty!

They say he was left-handed
and a rather quiet guy.
He liked to sit around and think...
Who? What? When? Where? And why?

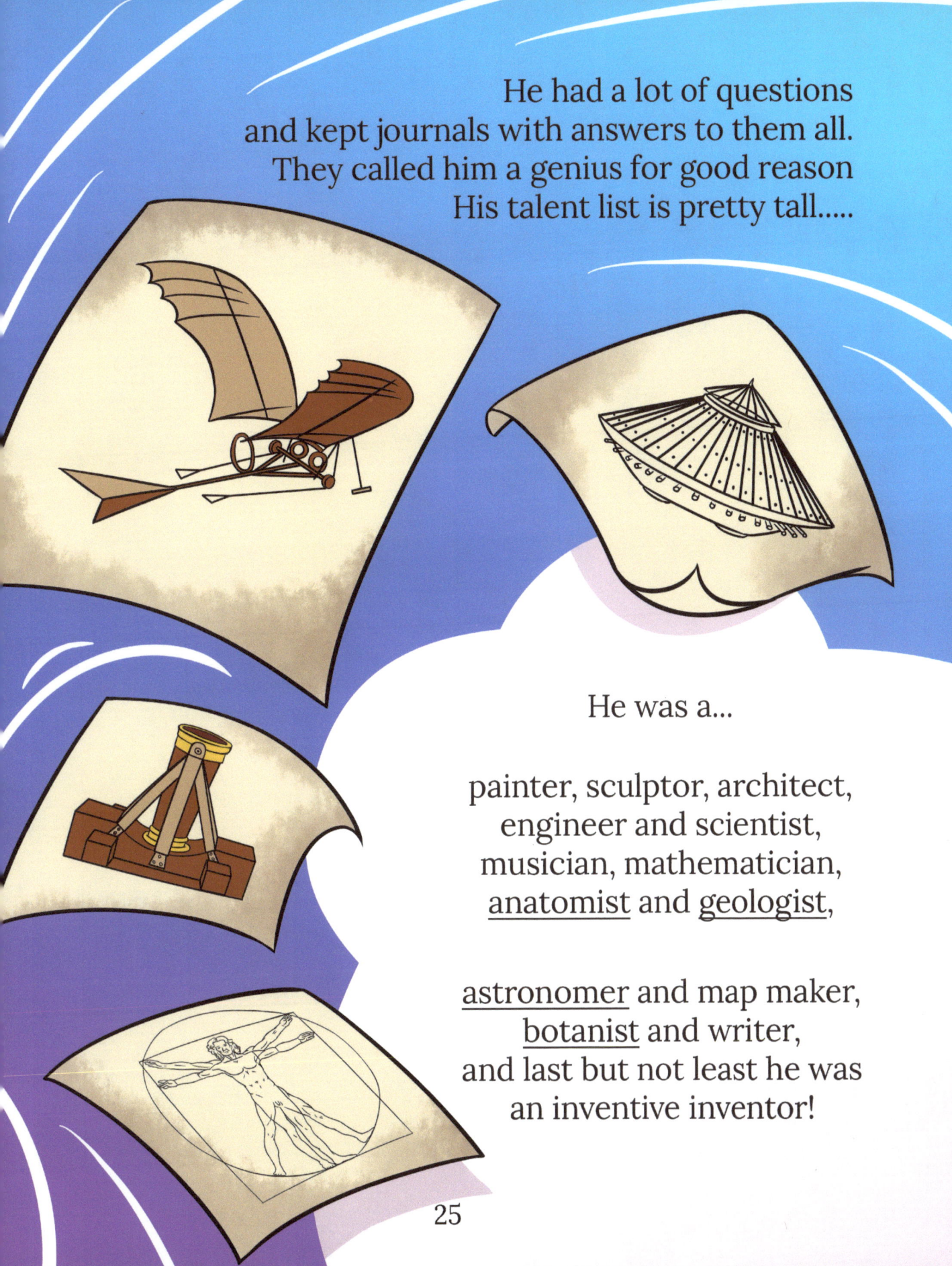

He had a lot of questions
and kept journals with answers to them all.
They called him a genius for good reason
His talent list is pretty tall......

He was a...

painter, sculptor, architect,
engineer and scientist,
musician, mathematician,
anatomist and geologist,

astronomer and map maker,
botanist and writer,
and last but not least he was
an inventive inventor!

It took almost 200 years before it was fully built. The Leaning Tower of Pisa, and boy, does it tilt!

Unfortunately, it's true. The experts are thinking that due to the soft ground it will keep right on sinking.

Let's head over to Cinque Terra,
The "5 lands," as they say,
named for the tiny towns
all lined up in this way.

We can walk through lemon <u>groves</u> and hike from town to town.
<u>Scale</u> the mountainside and waterfalls; see the views before heading back down.

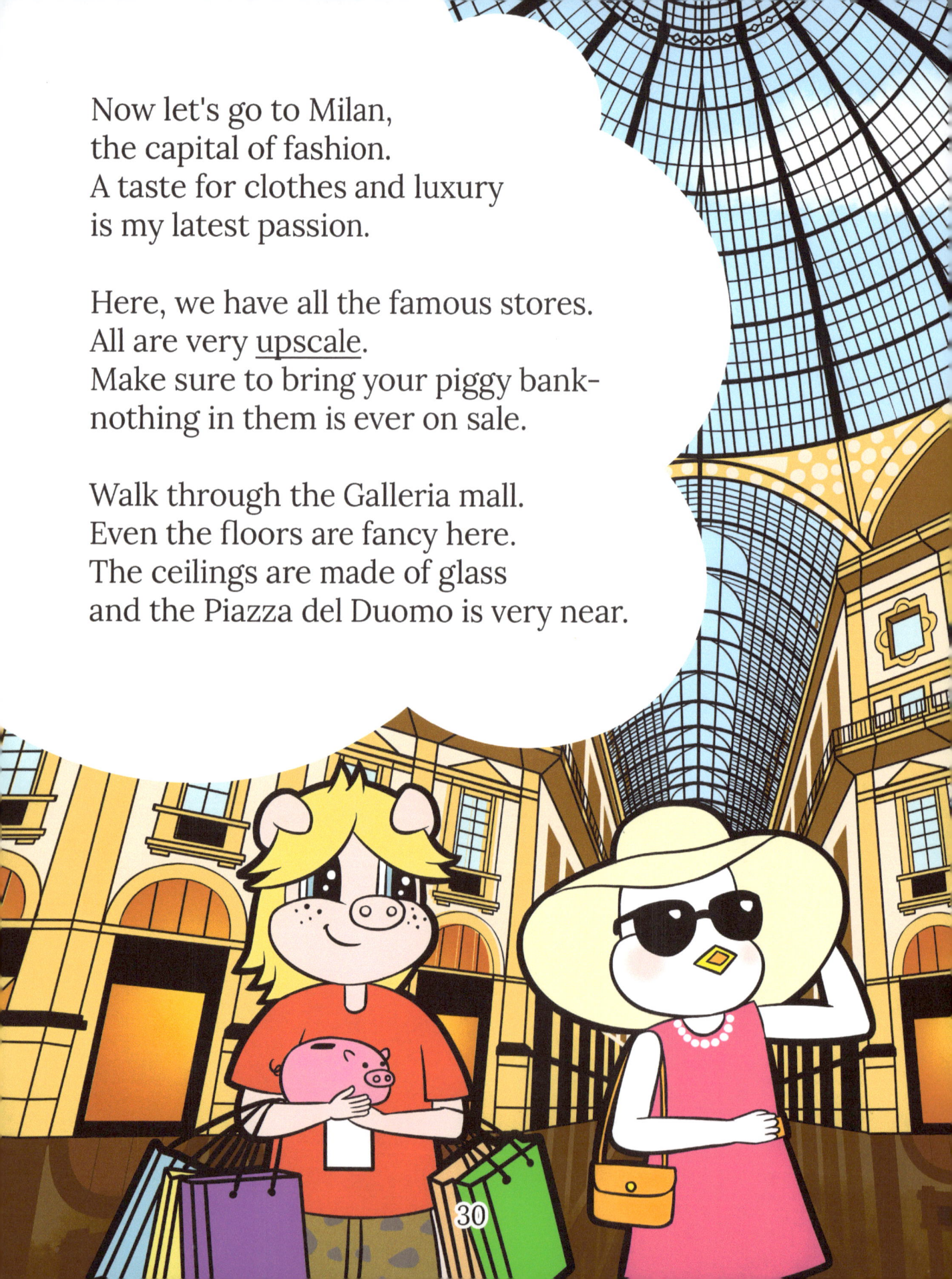

Now let's go to Milan,
the capital of fashion.
A taste for clothes and luxury
is my latest passion.

Here, we have all the famous stores.
All are very upscale.
Make sure to bring your piggy bank-
nothing in them is ever on sale.

Walk through the Galleria mall.
Even the floors are fancy here.
The ceilings are made of glass
and the Piazza del Duomo is very near.

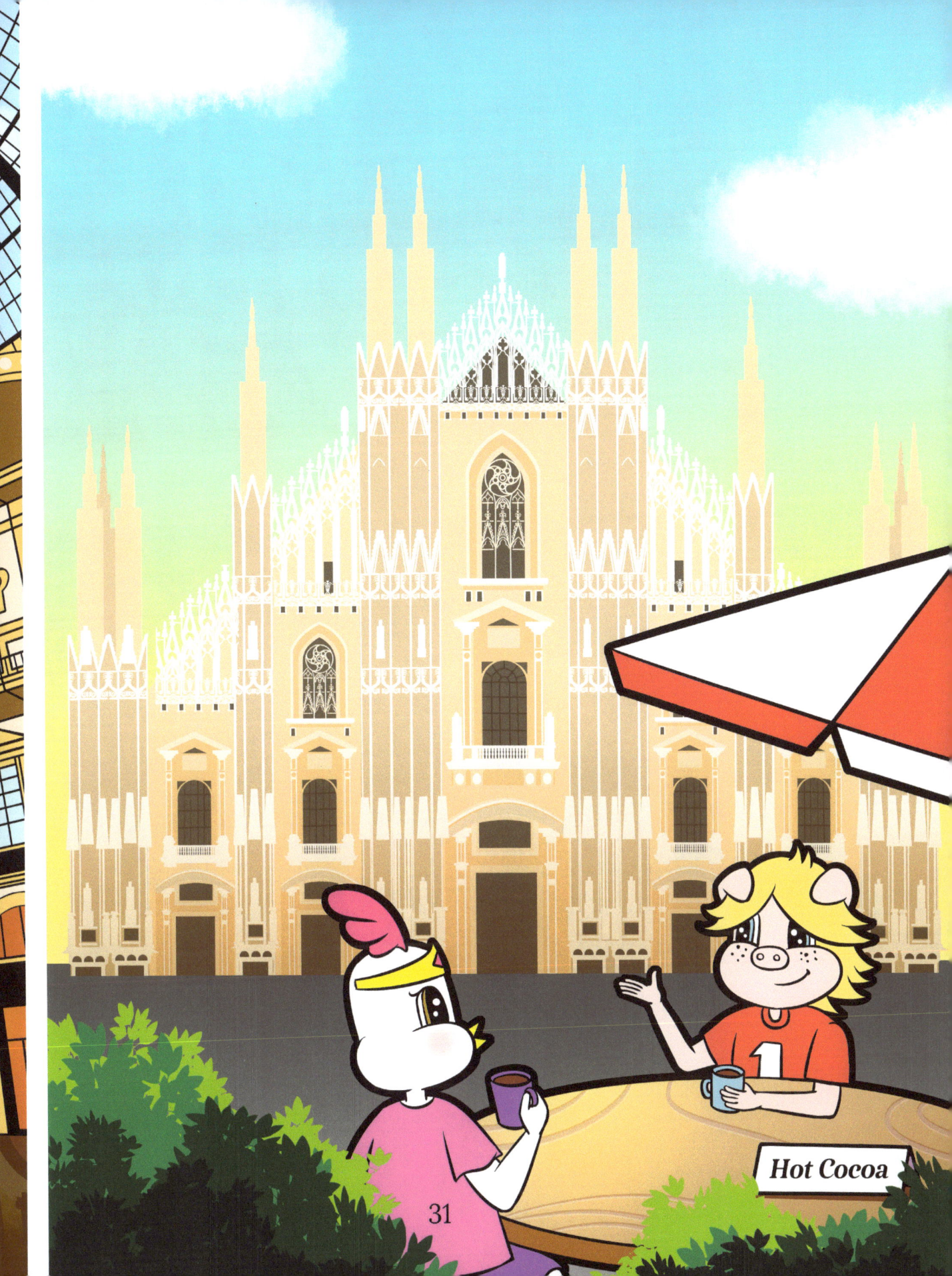

Venice is the city of canals.
According to my notes,
not too many cars are here.
Most get around in boats.

It's a group of small islands.
The canals twist in between,
linked by bridges big and small.
Look here, you'll see what I mean,

A gondola ride
is the best thing to do
at night, by moonlight,
as the gondoliers sing to you.

Next, we'll head straight down
to Italy's high heel.
In Puglia, we can find
our next delicious meal.

Horace, an <u>ancient</u> poet,
once wrote on his pad
that the bread here was
"far the best bread to be had."

DOP bread is famous.
I would really like some.
And just like Horace,
I will eat every crumb!

We can roam the streets
to see the cute little homes.
The Trulli Houses
look like they were built for gnomes.

They are lined up in rows
and are made out of stones.
The bottoms are <u>whitewashed</u>
and the tops look like cones.

A long, long time ago
back in 79 AD,
Mount Vesuvius <u>erupted</u>
sending <u>ash</u> to the sea.

Everything was covered.
The whole city of Pompeii
was <u>preserved</u> in its place
just like it was on that last day.

It was buried and lost
for more than one thousand years
until it was found again
by <u>excavation pioneers</u>.

A lot of work has been done
to dig out what was left behind.
It is just amazing
what they were able to find:

Homes, temples, roads, and stores--
an entire city well-designed!

There's so much <u>ancient</u> history here.
There's so much to see and do.
Let's go down to Sicily
and do what the Sicilians do.

The Valley of the Temples
is not in a valley at all.
It's really on a mountainside
amongst almond trees grown tall.

These ancient buildings
were built just to show
devotion to gods and goddesses
long, long ago.

The Greek Theater in Taormina
is really quite the treat.
You can see beautiful views
of the sea and Mt. Etna from your seat.

Out of Italy's three volcanoes,
Mt. Etna is the largest by a mile.
The soils it produces
makes the land very fertile.

It's one of the world's most active.
This is something we just learned:
The meaning of "Etna"
in Greek is "I burn."

Before we are through,
before we are all done,
let's talk about Italian culture.
They know how to have some fun!

Italian food is famous.
And really, we can see why.
Everything is super yummy.
Come on, give it a try!

Do you guys like noodles?
Yes, definitely!
So many shapes and sizes--
Ziti, spaghetti, and macaroni.

Noodles are called pasta here.
There are over 200 shapes, we hear.

What about pizza?
Pepperoni and cheese!!
Italian pizzas are delicious.
Would you like seconds?--Yes, please!!

We like to play a lot of sports.
Do you have a favorite game?
Italians love the game of soccer.
But they call it by a different name.

They love a good car race
and a day at the tracks.
The Ferrari is a winner
with lots of trophies and plaques.

Ciao, we must leave you.
Now we must go, you see.
Now, you can say
"<u>Veni, Vidi, Vici!</u>"
We are so glad you joined us
on our trip to Italy.

But there's something to remember
and please don't forget:
The more you learn of our world,
the smaller it can get.

The places can look different,
the people not like you,
but we all want the same in life:
Peace, Love, and Happiness-to name a few.

So when you go off traveling
to an amazing <u>destination</u>,
respect the people, culture, and land
and have an awesome vacation!

Map 1.

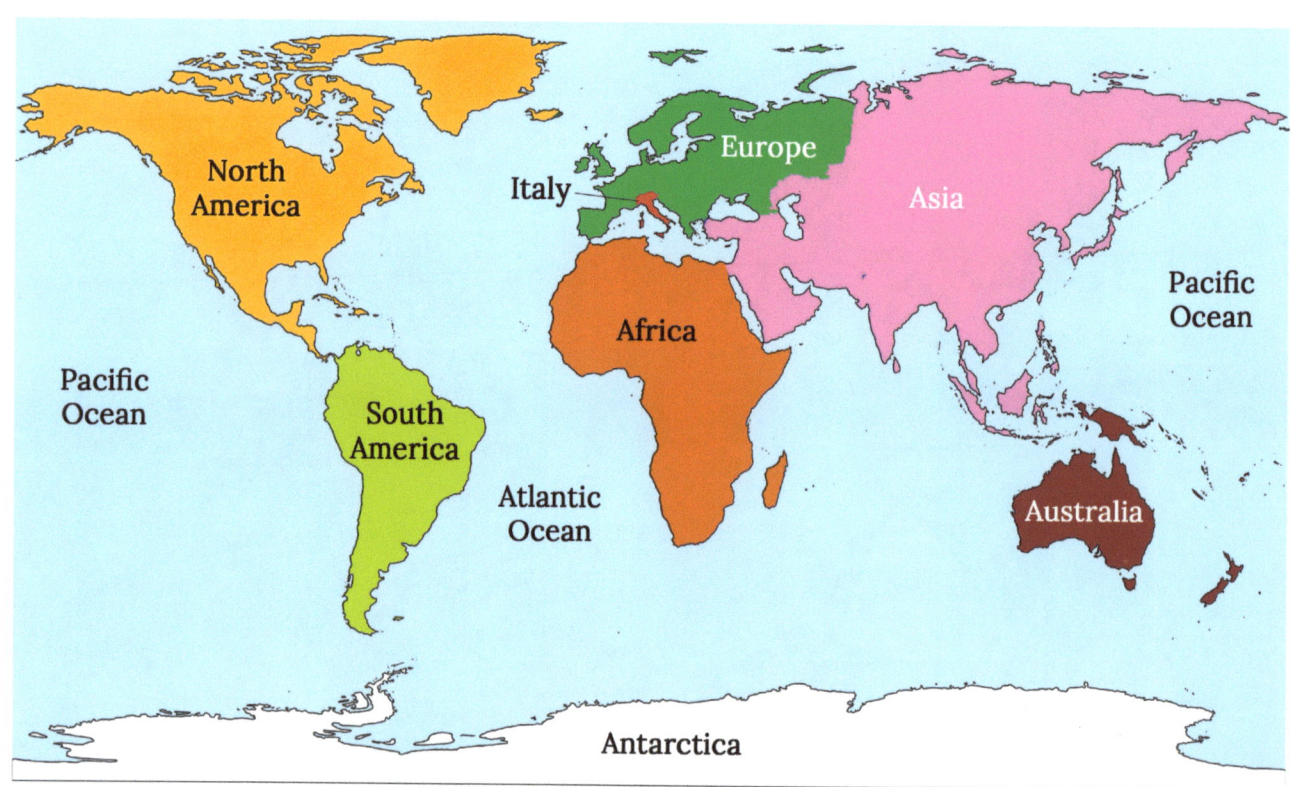

The continents of the world

Map 2.

GLOSSARY:

amphitheater: an open circular or oval building with a central space surrounded by rows of seats to watch a performance or sporting event

anatomist: a person who studies anatomy, or the parts of the body

ancient: really old

ash: the powder that is left after something has burned

astronomer: a person who studies astronomy, the study of space, the universe, the solar system, stars, the sun, etc

botanist: a person who studies plants

canals: a waterway that can lead inland and allow boats to travel through

citizens: the people who live in a particular place

destination: the place that you are going to

dueling: fighting or competing

erupted: sent out rocks, ash, lava, etc in a sudden explosion

excavation: a big dig

feat: accomplishment or achievement

fertile: rich or productive, able to produce healthy plants

finance: the way money is loaned, used, or borrowed. In this case, the Medici family paid, or "financed," for a lot of artwork and science advances during the Renaissance

geologist: a person who studies landforms and rocks and how they have changed over time

gladiators: men in ancient Rome who fought other men or animals often to the death to entertain other people

gondola: a long, narrow boat with a flat bottom

gondolier: a person who steers a gondola using a long pole

gravity: the force by which all objects in the universe are attracted to each other

grove: a small group of trees

Mass: a religious tradition in the Catholic Church

patrons: people who pay or support artists, scientists, organizations in order for them to create or work on advances in their fields

physics: the study of nature, matter, and energy. People who study physics often study light, radiation, sound, heat, mechanics, electricity, magnetism, and atoms

pioneers: people who begin or help start or go somewhere new and prepare the way for others to follow

plaques: flat, thin pieces of metal or wood with writing indicating something to remember like a historical event or an achievement

Pope: the leader of the Catholic Church

preserved: kept in good condition over a long period of time

printing press: a machine that prints books, magazines, and newspapers

Renaissance: this time period (from the 14th century to the 17th century in Europe) came about because people began changing their way of thinking. People wanted to learn more about the world around them which was the start of a new age of science. People wanted to be more creative and think out of the box which led to inventions, different architecture, and many artworks. People also began thinking about the meaning of life leading to advances in philosophy (the study of life, human nature, truth, knowledge)

republican/representative government: a kind of government in which its people elect, or choose, their leaders

ruins: the remaining pieces of something that was destroyed

scaffolding: a temporary structure made from metal or wood that a person can stand on to work high above the ground or floor

scale: climb up

Senate: a group of people who meet to discuss and make the laws of a country, state, or organization

upscale: fancy and expensive

Veni vidi vici: "I came, I saw, I conquered." Although it was first said by Julius Caesar after he won a battle, people often use this phrase when they accomplished something or saw something all the way through

whitewashed: painted white with paint, lime, or chalk

Acknowledgements:

Thank you Lei! As always, your patient and creative ways amaze me! Thank you kids for patiently waiting for your snacks while Mommy tries to get her rhymes to make sense! Thank you Nick for always encouraging me and believing my little books "have legs."

This book is dedicated to Salty. You were the most loyal and forgiving dog on the planet. We lost you in 2020 making that year even harder. I hope you are running the beach, surfing the waves, and dock jumping to your heart's delight in Doggy Heaven.
We love you, bud.

© RMN-Grand Palais / Michel Urtado / Art Resource, NY

Copyright © 2021 by Kimberly Naylor
Illustrated by Lei Yang
All rights reserved.

Travel Bug Press 2021
ISBN: 978-0-9979493-5-3

www.ingramcontent.com/pod-product-compliance
Lightning Source LLC
LaVergne TN
LVHW071026070426
835507LV00002B/43